Sunny

By Juniata Rogers

The sky is clear. The air is warm. It is a lovely sunny day!

The sun shines through some palm trees.

Earth is the third planet from the Sun.

The sun is about 93 million miles (150 million km) away. Its rays cross all those miles to send heat and light to Earth.

The sun powers ocean **currents**. It makes the wind. Even rain begins with a sunny day.

Rainbows happen when sunlight hits raindrops.

Water condenses over a lake.

Rain comes from Earth's water. The sun heats water into a **gas**. The gas rises into the sky and cools. It **condenses** into water droplets that form clouds.

The droplets get bigger and fall as rain. The rainwater flows into rivers, lakes, and oceans. The sun warms the water and the cycle begins again.

Some areas of the world get more rain than others.

Like all plants, corn needs sunlight to grow.

Sunny days grow Earth's plants. Plants make energy from the sun. Animals eat the plants. Other animals eat the plant-eaters! All life on Earth can trace its energy back to sunshine.

Sunny places can use the sun for power. **Solar cells** and solar power plants turn sunshine into electricity.

Solar cells can be big or small.

Droughts can happen all over the world.

Sunny days aren't always good. A **drought** occurs when a place does not receive enough rain. During a drought, plants may die. There may not be enough water to drink.

Time in the sun is good for us. But too much sun can mean a **sunburn**. Sunscreen prevents sunburn by blocking the sun's rays.

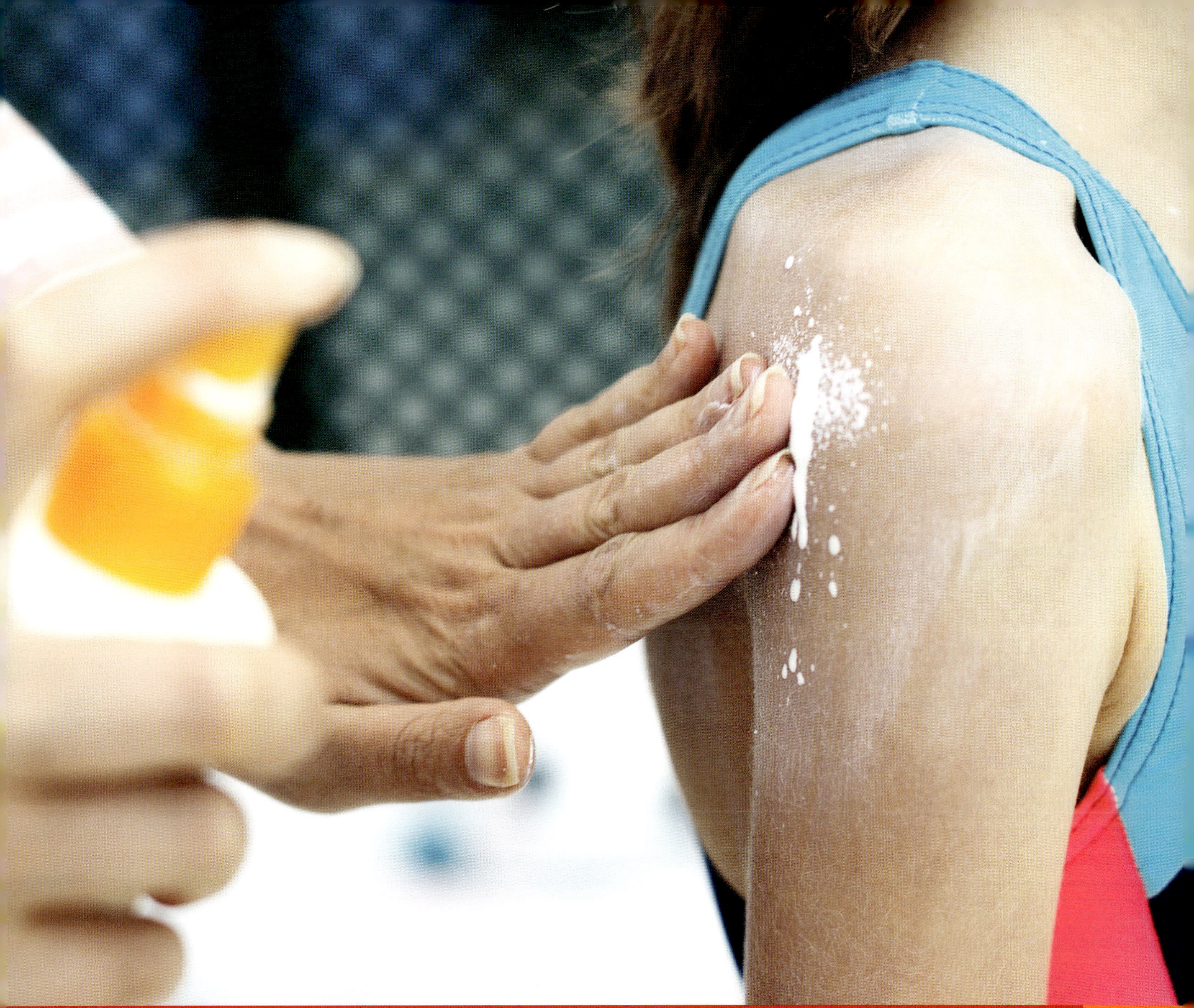

Be sure to put on sunscreen before going to the beach.

There are so many things to do in the sunshine!

Where do you have fun in the sun? The beach? The park? You may be playing, but the sun is hard at work!

Glossary

condense (kun-DENTS): When a gas cools and becomes liquid, it condenses.

currents (KUR-rents): Currents are flows of water in a river or ocean. In the ocean, currents always take the same basic paths.

drought (DROWT): A period of time when an area does not get as much rain as it normally does, causing a shortage in the water supply.

gas (GAS): What liquid becomes when it heats up. Gas does not have a shape. It spreads out as far as possible.

solar cells (SOL-ur SELZ): Machine-made panels that use sunshine to make electricity.

sunburn (SUN-burn): When skin is in the sun for too long, it burns. It turns red, painful, and hot to the touch.

To Find Out More

Books

Branley, Dr. Franklyn M. *Sunshine Makes the Seasons*. New York, NY: Harper, 2016.

Kudlinski, Kathleen V. *Boy, Were We Wrong About the Weather!* New York, NY: Dial Books for Young Readers, 2015.

Taylor-Butler, Christine. *The Sun*. New York, NY: Children's Press, 2014.

Websites

Visit our website for links about sunshine:
childsworld.com/links

Note to Parents, Teachers, and Librarians: We routinely verify our Web links to make sure they are safe and active sites. So encourage your readers to check them out!

Index

About the Author

Juniata Rogers grew up in Newport, Rhode Island. She has worked as a naturalist, an art model, and a teacher. She's been writing professionally for 25 years, and currently lives near Washington, DC.

The Child's World
childsworld.com

Published by The Child's World®
1980 Lookout Drive • Mankato, MN 56003-1705
800-599-READ • www.childsworld.com

Photo credits: Brian A Jackson/Shutterstock.com: 11; Danie Nel Photography/Shutterstock.com: 15; Dmitri Ma/Shutterstock.com: 19; Mike Mareen/Shutterstock.com: 7; mironov/Shutterstock.com: 8; nevodka/Shutterstock.com: 3; Piyaset/Shutterstock.com: 16; Smileus/Shutterstock.com: 12; Subbotina Anna/Shutterstock.com: 20; Valeri Potapova/Shutterstock.com: 4; XiXinXing/Shutterstock.com: cover, 1

ISBN Hardcover: 9781503827929
ISBN Paperback: 9781622434602
LCCN: 2018939772

Printed in the United States of America • PA02398